STUDENT BODY
(High School Edition)

Frank Winters

D0933233

BROADWAY PLAY PUBLISHING INC
224 E 62nd St, NY, NY 10065
www.broadwayplaypub.com
info@broadwayplaypub.com

STUDENT BODY (High School Edition)
© Copyright 2016 by Frank Winters

First printing: July 2016
I S B N: 978-0-88145-673-8
Book design: Marie Donovan
Typographic controls: Adobe InDesign
Typeface: Palatino
Printed and bound in the U S A

AUTHOR'S NOTE

When this play was first commissioned by The Strasberg Institute, it was for a group of young actors, and so I set it in high school. When it was subsequently produced at The Flea Theatre, we decided to make the characters a few years older, as their resident acting company, The Bats, were mostly in their middle or late 20s. The shift of the setting from high school to college required a reimagining of a number of characters, relationships, and group dynamics. Beyond that, each version of the play reflects the work of the different actors, designers and production teams this play enjoyed, particularly that of directors Michelle Tattenbaum, Danny Sharron, and associate director Alex Keegan. So, now we have these two utterly similar, yet wildly different plays, existing in alternate realities right next to each other within the multiverse of the American Theater. Enjoy.

STUDENT BODY (High School Edition) (under the title THE SCHOOL PLAY) was originally commissioned, developed and performed at the Lee Strasberg Theatre and Film Institute in New York City as part of the Clifford Odets Ensemble Play Commission in December 2014. The cast and creative contributors were:

APRIL	Remington Moses
LUCY	Amanda Stewart
MALCOLM	Zack Kozlow
NATALIE	Stephanie Rose Wurster
LIZ	Drita Kabashi
ROB	Jeremy Stewart
PETE	Daniel Manning
DAISY	Lauren Mui
MAGGIE	Yeujia Low
SARAH	Danielle Guido
Director	Danny Sharron
Scenic designer	Rebecca Phillips
Lighting designer	Miriam Nilofa Crowe
Costume designer	Angela Harner
Sound designer	Michael Costagliola
Fight director	Mitch McCoy
Associate director	Alex Keegan
Assistant lighting designer	Korey-Elizabeth Rushing-Parker
Production manager	Karina Martins
Technical director	Jenn Tash
Stage manager	Kyle Ferguson
Assistant stage manager	Elizabeth Ramsay

Marketing ....Aaron Schroeder
Publicity................................Sam Rudy, Miguel Mendiola
Front of house ....Jerry Sheehan, Samantha Castro,
Dori Sullivan

CHARACTERS & SETTING

APRIL
DAISY
LUCY
MALCOLM
NATALIE
LIZ
PETE
ROB
MAGGIE
SARAH

A high school auditorium in Craigstown, Indiana

AUTHOR'S OTHER NOTE

Use of the "/" means this is where the next line begins,
overlapping with the preceding line's dialogue.

(Lights up. We open on a high school auditorium in Craigstown, Indiana.)

(On stage, the set is half-finished. Next week, they'll be doing something like "Hello, Dolly!" But for now, the theater is dark, the ground cluttered with the detritus of tech week.)

(All that we can really make out is a ghost light, a white bulb sitting atop a tall, thin, standing lamp on wheels that casts a weak, pale glow around it. April, a stage manager, enters, listening to something like "Take Me or Leave Me" from Rent *through her headphones.)*

(Just as she steps onstage, she receives a text message. She stops, reads it, and there, all alone in the darkness, April beams.)

LUCY: *(O S)* Hello?

(LUCY enters and APRIL begins setting up the space for what is to come, surreptitiously pocketing her phone.)

APRIL: Lucy? Where are you, can you see?

LUCY: I see a bright, white light. Am I dying?

APRIL: No, it's just a ghost light.

LUCY: Are you sure? Because that sounds like something you'd see if you were dying.

APRIL: Sarah called you?

LUCY: Yeah, what in the hell is going on right now?

APRIL: I have no idea, Sarah called me, said she needed some place where we can all talk without being interrupted, so I volunteered here.

LUCY: The school?

APRIL: The theater.

LUCY: And what do you mean, "without being interrupted."

APRIL: She wouldn't say.

LUCY: She called me like an hour ago, wouldn't tell me anything, just said to meet her here at midnight which is weird, right?

APRIL: Pretty weird.

LUCY: And she sounded weird, right? I mean.

APRIL: Weird like how?

LUCY: Like freaked?

APRIL: Maybe a little? But I'm sure it's fine.

LUCY: You think?

APRIL: It's Sarah Ferguson. How bad can it be? / Oh, and I have something for you...

(APRIL *reaches into her bag and hands* LUCY *a bottle of whiskey—expensive looking.*)

LUCY: Well, I hope you're right because for whatever it's worth I am exactly the kind of girl who gets killed first in a horror movie and / whaaaaaat. No way. You're an angel.

APRIL: It's the right kind, right?

LUCY: It's perfect. You're perfect. Thank you, April.

APRIL: Well, don't thank me, thank Cal. It was his fake.

(APRIL *hands* LUCY *a receipt and some change.*)

LUCY: And you didn't tell him what it was for, right? Or who?

APRIL: I just said it was for a "friend."

LUCY: It's perfect. This is his favorite, not even so much for drinking, but because there's this guy in this movie.

(APRIL *returns to the business of straightening out the room* as LUCY *admires her bottle.*)

APRIL: I'm glad. We had to try two different places. Guy didn't even know he had it. Cal had to point it out to him and it was this whole big thing and what? (*She stops.*)

LUCY: What? Nothing.

APRIL: You made a face.

LUCY: No, I was just.

APRIL: You were just… / what?

LUCY: Is something…I don't know.

APRIL: What?

LUCY: Is something going on between you and Cal?

APRIL: What? No. (*She starts moving again.*)

LUCY: I'm just asking, you guys just seem to spend a lot of time / hanging out together and he talks about you a lot—

APRIL: Well, yeah, because we're friends and there is nothing going on and wait, what did he say about me?

MALCOLM: (*O S*) Hello?

(LUCY *turns around, quickly stashes the bottle in her bag.* APIL *plays pass interference.*)

APRIL: Hey, Malcolm.

MALCOLM: Hey, April.

APRIL: Did it start snowing yet?

MALCOLM: Any minute now. Heard it might be a blizzard.

APRIL: Really?

MALCOLM: Guy said ten to twelve inches.

APRIL: I love a good snow storm. It's like the whole world's in this big pillow fort and—

LUCY: Hey, Malcolm.

(LUCY *turns back to face him and suddenly she is all he sees. They're both terribly in love.*)

MALCOLM: (*Suddenly with stars in his eyes*) Oh, hey. Hey, Lucy.

LUCY: Hey.

(Um)

APRIL: Well, I'm gonna go head up to the booth so I can—

(They're not listening)

APRIL: Kay. Bye. *(She exits, unnoticed.)*

LUCY: Hey.

MALCOLM: Hey. So, this is weird, huh?

LUCY: Tell me about it.

MALCOLM: Any word on what this is, yet? It's not like a *Carrie* thing, is it?

LUCY: Sarah just said to meet here at midnight. That's all I know.

MALCOLM: You know, I didn't even have Sarah in my phone. Almost didn't pick up.

LUCY: But you figured, mysterious phone call, midnight, in a darkened theater…

MALCOLM: What could possibly go wrong?

LUCY: Exactly.

MALCOLM: I guess we'll have to wait and see. Speaking of which.

LUCY: Yeah?

MALCOLM: Can anyone, you know, see us nmff—?

(LUCY *grabs* MALCOLM *by the collar and kisses him. And he melts.*)

MALCOLM: Happy Anniversary.

LUCY: Happy Anniversary.

MALCOLM: That's insane.

LUCY: I know, it's like a whole *year's* aversary.

(LUCY *and* MALCOLM *kiss again. He initiates this time. Then:*)

MALCOLM: Hey, I got you something.

LUCY: What? But I thought we said.

MALCOLM: Yeah, well, I got you something anyway.

LUCY: Whaaaaaat. You dick. *I totally got you something, too.*

MALCOLM: Really?

LUCY: Yeah, can I go first?

MALCOLM: Yeah, just, can I say something?

LUCY: Is it mushy?

MALCOLM: There is a factor of mush.

LUCY: Then, yeah, say it.

MALCOLM: Wait, let's go outside.

LUCY: What? Why?

MALCOLM: Because I don't want to do it in here. Somebody might.

LUCY: We're all alone. Plenty private.

MALCOLM: We're on a stage.

LUCY: What did you want to say to me?

MALCOLM: Well—

(*The lights come on as the door opens—*)

NATALIE: *(O S)* WE HAVE ARRIVED. / WE ARE HERE. NOBODY PANIC.

LUCY: Motherfucker.

(NATALIE *enters with* LIZ. MALCOLM *and* LUCY *trade looks; shit, this might have to wait. We see how instantly the presence of other people makes* MALCOLM *shrink into minor. They stop touching, yet the connection between them remains taut and ever-present.)*

LUCY: Hello?

NATALIE: Oh, hey girl.

LUCY: Natalie?

NATALIE: Whadup.

LUCY: You a li'l drunk?

(Yup)

NATALIE: No. Why? Are you?

LUCY: No.

NATALIE: *(Suddenly mid-interrogation)* Who did this to you. You tell me who did this to you.

LUCY: I'm, no. I'm not.

NATALIE: Well, good, because I'm not afraid to tell you there, Lucy Liu.

LIZ: I got her keys. *(She is her group's designated driver; she's on her second cup of take out coffee and the night is still young.)*

NATALIE: I'm not gonna lie to you there, that there was a period of time where it was touch and go there for a mit. A binnit. A bit of a minute.

LUCY: Is she on something?

NATALIE: *Nailed it.*

LIZ: Tequila?

NATALIE: TEQUILA.

LIZ: She wanted to get wasted, so we called Rob and Pete who created a game with a series of rules that would last all night by which every time a rule is broken, she has to take a drink.

LUCY: Well, what are the rules?

LIZ: They won't tell anybody.

LUCY: Excellent. Well. Listen, I was just gonna run to the car to grab something, Malcolm, did you maybe…?

LIZ: Oh, hey, Malcolm. I didn't see you there.

MALCOLM: Yeah, hey.

(NATALIE *takes center stage.*)

NATALIE: Okay, I like this. This is nice. Are we doing a play?

LUCY: No.

NATALIE: What was I saying?

LIZ: You were about to tell the nice lady why you're trashed.

LUCY: You've got a reason? What's the reason?

NATALIE: I never needed a reason before.

LIZ: Yeah, but she has one. And it's good, right?

NATALIE: Hm? Oh. OH. That's right, I do, yes, I do. I do, but don't you say a word, okay? Do not say anything.

LUCY: I don't know anything.

NATALIE: I was talking to her.

LUCY: *But you were looking at me?*

LIZ: Why don't you just tell them?

LUCY: Tell me what? Wait. What's going on?

(APRIL *returns.*)

APRIL: Hey, can we all keep our voices down?

LIZ: Sorry.

LUCY: We're celebrating.

APRIL: Celebrating what?

LUCY: They won't tell me.

NATALIE: Hey, April's here, you guys!

LUCY: Speaking of which, I was just about to run out to the car, and, Malcolm? Did you wanna...?

NATALIE: Wait, you guys, you guys, wait, I'm trying to tell you my news.

LUCY: Which is what?

APRIL: Wait. What's going on?

LUCY: Natalie has news, apparently.

APRIL: She does? What is it?

(Beat. NATALIE *looks around. Then:)*

NATALIE: Hm?

LIZ: She got into college.

NATALIE: You asshole.

LUCY: You what?! Natalie, that's amazing.

NATALIE: You fucking son of a bitch piece of shit asshole.

LIZ: Like you were ever / gonna get there.

APRIL: Natalie, that's so great. Congratulations.

LUCY: You were early decision, right?

LIZ: To Northwestern.

LUCY: Congratulations.

NATALIE: Thank you. I'm in. I'm done. *(Correcting herself)* It's done. *I'm* very excited. You are dead to me.

LIZ: But that wasn't even the best part of the news, was it? Why don't you tell them the best part of the news?

LUCY: It wasn't?

APRIL: What's the best part of the news?

NATALIE: It wasn't? IT WASN'T. Oh my God oh my God no the best part is—

APRIL: And can she be like this all the time, please?

NATALIE: Oh. Oh. Oh. I don't have to pay anything!

(And from the edge of the theater, ROB blows a party horn— and PETE cheers.)

LUCY: What?! No.

LIZ: Full ride.

APRIL: What?!

LUCY: That's amazing. Your mom must be freaking out.

PETE: Amazing, right? So cool.

LUCY: You must be so relieved. And relaxed.

ROB: Relaxed is one word for it. Also inebriated.

LUCY: Also amazing.

ROB: Ahp. You gotta drink.

PETE: He's right.

ROB: We don't make the rules.

PETE: But you do have to drink.

NATALIE: Yeah, you're probably right. *(She takes a sip from her flask.)*

APRIL: So, wait, what are the rules?

ROB: Well, they're a secret.

APRIL: A secret to whom?

ROB: I lied.

PETE: We do make the rules.

ROB: But we can't tell you.

APRIL: Why?

ROB: Because the rules, I'm sorry to say, are known only to Calvin, Peter, and myself, and not just anybody gets to play. It's an honor, of sorts.

PETE: Special occasions.

ROB: Ahp. Y'see?

PETE: What?

ROB: You did it again.

NATALIE: I did?

PETE: You're right.

ROB: I know.

PETE: You're so right.

ROB: Drink.

NATALIE: I mean, you make a good point, so. *(She drinks.)*

LUCY: I am so lost.

APRIL: Well, congratulations, Natalie, you deserve it. Assuming you survive the night, I think you've got a bright future ahead of you.

(ROB blows the party horn again.)

LUCY: Okay, so, somebody's taking that away from him, right?

(ROB blows the party horn in her face, LUCY goes to snatch it away, and they struggle, laugh about it, which MALCOLM does not love.)

APRIL: Can we keep our voices down a little bit, please?

LIZ: Are we not supposed to be in here?

APRIL: It's a grey area.

PETE: Do we know who else is coming?

LIZ: Just Sarah, I guess.

APRIL: And Daisy.

ROB: *(Perking up)* Sarah called Daisy?

APRIL: Please be nice.

ROB: I'm always nice. I love Daisy. That's why I go to her Dunkin' Donuts every weekend, for her very angry, very anti-social bagels.

APRIL: You know, you guys are a lot alike, you know. / I'm serious.

ROB: Please don't say things like that.

APRIL: I'm just saying, I've known Daisy since forever and I think if you two stopped trying to bite each other's heads off for like, two seconds…

LIZ: She's got a point. There is some serious will they won't they tension there.

ROB: Please. Please stop. My brain?

MALCOLM: Actually, Lucy, did you still want to—

ROB: Oh, hey, Malcolm. I didn't see you back there.

LIZ: That's what I said.

MALCOLM: I, um.

ROB: Yeah, that's a cool story, bro. So, wait, so what is this, then? Do we know? Do any of us know what Sarah wants?

(LUCY and MALCOLM make eye contact through the crowd and suddenly, everything's okay.)

APRIL: Sarah called me, said she needed some place we could all talk without being interrupted, so I volunteered here.

ROB: And how can you get in here?

APRIL: Miss Haskins gave me a key for tech week.

PETE: And Sarah didn't tell you why?

APRIL: Nope.

LUCY: Me neither.

LIZ: Don't look at me.

PETE: Cool, so we're all definitely gonna die here tonight.

LIZ: You guys think we're in a horror movie?

LUCY: That's what I said.

ROB: You think it's about the party?

APRIL: We are not having a party in here. I cannot stress that enough.

ROB: I meant Sarah's party, her little…

APRIL: And we are also not gonna talk about that, okay?

ROB: I was just saying, if, for whatever reason, she felt compelled to…

LIZ: You're like a guy in an eighties movie, you know that? Both of you. You're like the guy who beats up Marty McFly.

PETE: Hey, he has a name. It's Biff. And he's awesome. And take that back.

ROB: Well, whatever it is, we need to get it over with fast, because this one still has a long night ahead of her.

PETE: Plus, the roads are gonna be a mess in a few hours and we still have to meet Cal over at Mike's thing.

APRIL: Oh, can I tag along?

ROB: Depends. Can we party in here?

APRIL: No.

ROB: Then we may need to work out some kind of a barter system?

LUCY: You guys are aware that we could all just kill you and then not say anything, right?

ROB: And how is that the sexiest thing you've ever said?

(DAISY *enters.*)

DAISY: Hello?

APRIL: Daisy? Hey, we're all over here. (*She gets up and rushes to meet her.*)

DAISY: April?

APRIL: Hey, you came!

DAISY: I said I was.

APRIL: Did it start snowing yet? You look frozen.

DAISY: Yeah, I had to walk. / Is this everybody?

APRIL: You had to walk?

DAISY: Sheila's in the shop. Is this everybody?

APRIL: Still waiting on Sarah. It's good to see you.

DAISY: And still no idea what's going on?

APRIL: Not yet. Everybody's just hanging out. Very casual. (*Softly*) Y'see? I told you it wouldn't be weird.

ROB: Oh, hey, Daisy.

APRIL: Remember you love me.

ROB: You wanna come over, join in our reindeer games?

DAISY: (*Putting her headphones in*) So hard. (*She finds a place by the wall where she pulls out her phone.*)

PETE: Okay, and I just want to be clear, right, that none of us count it none of us know what we're doing here, in a dark room, in the middle of the night?

LIZ: Correct.

PETE: *(Incensed)* Has Wes Craven taught us nothing, people?

MAGGIE: Hello? / Sorry, I. *(She stands in the doorway.)*

LIZ: Maggie?

MAGGIE: Hey, Liz.

LIZ: Maggie, what are you doing here?

MAGGIE: Sarah called me.

LIZ: Did you tell mom where you were?

MAGGIE: No.

LIZ: So, where does she think you are?

APRIL: It's fine, Liz.

LIZ: Where did you tell mom you were going?

MAGGIE: Mom doesn't care. I said I was going over Sarah's.

LIZ: In the middle of the night?

MAGGIE: It's fine.

LIZ: How did you even get here?

MAGGIE: I took the bus.

LIZ: You took the bus?

MAGGIE: So?

LIZ: My mother, ladies and gentlemen.

MAGGIE: So, what?

LIZ: So, you're gonna get your stupid ass kidnapped and then murdered and then I'm gonna have to pay ransom for your stupid ass and then.

PETE: Wait, isn't her stupid ass dead in this scenario?

LIZ: Shut up, Biff.

APRIL: It's fine, Liz, she's here. No harm done.

ROB: Oh, hey, Maggie.

MAGGIE: *(Puppy love in her eyes)* Hey, Rob.

LIZ: And you didn't say anything to mom about where I was, right?

MAGGIE: I didn't even know you were gonna be here. Honest. Sarah just said to show up at twelve.

ROB: Maggie, you and Sarah are close, right?

MAGGIE: I mean.

ROB: You wouldn't happen to know what we're all doing here by any chance, would you?

MAGGIE: Well, if Sarah's not here.

LIZ: Wait. Did she tell you?

APRIL: Guys.

MAGGIE: I mean, we only talked for a little.

APRIL: Guys.

ROB: Should we call her?

MAGGIE: She's on her way, I'm sure.

PETE: So, you do know why we're here?

APRIL: Guys. It's fine. You don't have to say anything if you don't want to. We'll just have to wait. Right?

PETE: Fine.

ROB: Cool.

APRIL: Thank you.

(Beat)

PETE: Okay, so if this was a horror movie, who'd be the first to die?

(SARAH enters in a barely suppressed panic.)

SARAH: Sorry I'm so sorry I'm late. It started snowing like ten seconds ago but the roads were already icy and I had to wait for, sorry, April, can I…?

APRIL: You want to shut it?

SARAH: I was hoping to lock it?

PETE: And danger, Will Robinson.

ROB: For real.

PETE: Sarah?

SARAH: Yeah?

PETE: You're not gonna, like, shoot everybody or anything, are you?

SARAH: What?

APRIL: It's fine, Sarah, the door automatically locks on the outside. Did you push the little thing?

SARAH: No.

APRIL: Push the little thing.

SARAH: Okay.

PETE: So, am I not getting an answer to my question?

(*She pushes the little thing.* SARAH *shuts the door, heads for the stage.*)

SARAH: Look, I know this is all really bizarre and weird but I think in a few minutes, you'll understand why with all the cloak and is she okay?

LIZ: (*Re:* NATALIE, *who has found her way to the floor.*) She's fine. She's matriculating.

SARAH: Okay.

LUCY: So, this is everybody, right?

ROB: Yeah, and how long is this gonna take, you think?

SARAH: Shouldn't take long.

ROB: Good. Because the night is young and some of us still have some pretty terrible life choices to make, so if you wouldn't mind…?

PETE: Well said.

LUCY: What's up?

SARAH: Well, first of all, I just wanted to say thanks again for coming here tonight, and on such late notice, too, and with the snow. I, uh. Um. (*She looks out at her friends and is suddenly keenly aware that she is the youngest in the room. She freezes for a moment, uncertain. Beat.*)

NATALIE: (*Whispering, to* LIZ) Are we taking a moment of silence or something? / Did somebody die?

LIZ: (*Giggling, whispered*) Shh.

SARAH: So, I found this tape. (*Beat*) See, my dad, he got this camera for Christmas, which isn't important, but he never uses it, which is, and it's a nice camera, too, so I figured maybe I should use it to take some pictures of the party, which I didn't, obviously, because as you may recall I passed out pretty early.

ROB: Which was / awesome.

SARAH: Humiliating, right, and so, anyway, I passed out and then the party as you guys remember went on for a couple of hours afterwards and I guess throughout the night, different people had it, used it, and for the most part, it's just people being gross, but then it must have been towards the end of the night, it didn't look like there was a lot of people left, but there's something else, and I don't really know how to.

LUCY: What is it?

SARAH: A girl. (*Beat*) And she's on my kitchen table and there's a bunch of guys, and they're standing around her and you can't really make out most of the faces or anything but she's on the table and she's not wearing

any, um, clothes or anything, and there's this guy,
who.

APRIL: Sarah—

LIZ: Woah woah woah wait a sec.

SARAH: And it looks like, I mean, there were a bunch of
people watching, and and and yelling, and she isn't…
I mean, you can't always see it quite right but at a
certain point, it doesn't even look like she's…

LIZ: Like she's what?

SARAH: Conscious?

APRIL: Oh, my God.

SARAH: And you can't hear, like, screaming or
anything, but it also kinda looks like somebody might
be holding her, um, her ankles?

LIZ: Holding her or holding her down?

SARAH: Well, that's the thing, actually.

LIZ: Holding her or holding her down?

SARAH: Well, no, that's the thing. / You can't exactly
tell.

LIZ: Oh, that's the thing? And what do you mean, you
can't tell?

SARAH: I mean, I can't tell if what's going on if it's
just, you know, sex on my kitchen table which would
honestly be bad enough, or, or if it's something else.

PETE: Something like what?

SARAH: Something worse.

APRIL: Sarah.

SARAH: And I was gonna bring it straight to the
cops, you know, but, then I thought, well, what if it's
nothing? What if it only looks like it's something bad
and people get in trouble anyway and?

ROB: No, that's smart.

SARAH: So, I brought it here. To you.

APRIL: Why us?

SARAH: Because you're my friends, you're my friends and you were there, and, you know, conscious, and—

MALCOLM: Well, actually, I, uh. Wasn't.

ROB: You weren't conscious?

MALCOLM: I wasn't there.

SARAH: Yes, you were. We talked.

MALCOLM: On the porch, yeah, but I never came inside.

SARAH: Why not?

MALCOLM: *(An eye on* ROB*)* No particular reason.

LIZ: Excellent.

SARAH: I'm sorry about this, Malcolm.

MALCOLM: It's okay.

SARAH: But, maybe you've heard something then, or, I don't know, have any of you heard anything? Do any of you have any idea of what I'm talking about? At all?

(Everybody looks around. Beat. Then:)

ROB: I, uh…?

PETE: Sorry, Sarah.

ROB: Yeah. Sorry.

LIZ: I haven't heard anything.

APRIL: Me neither.

*(*LUCY *shrugs.)*

SARAH: Nothing?

NATALIE: Hm?

SARAH: Well, then I need your help.

PETE: What do you mean?

SARAH: I mean, I found this tape and I don't know what to do with it.

PETE: So, what do you want us to do?

SARAH: Tell me what to do with it.

LIZ: Okay, and this is where I jump off. / Natalie, come on, get up. I'm taking you home.

SARAH: Wait a minute, what? Liz. / Where are you going?

(LIZ *starts getting her stuff together.*)

LIZ: Maggie, get your coat. Rob, Pete, if you need a ride either speak now or forever hold your peace / otherwise you can always take the bus.

ROB: Liz, why are you freaking out?

LIZ: I'm not freaking out. I am just leaving right now before we do something stupid, the storm hits, and we end up like the Donner Party. Are you coming?

ROB: Sarah asked for our help.

LIZ: Of course she did. She's terrified. Like you should be. / Maggie?

ROB: Why should I be terrified?

LIZ: Did you not hear any of what she just said? She's got a video of kids from our school assaulting another kid from our school at a party that we all were at.

ROB: She thinks.

LIZ: Well, I don't want any part of this.

ROB: We don't even know what this is yet.

LIZ: Oh, come on.

ROB: We don't.

LIZ: Okay, look. Fine. You want me to settle this for you? Sarah, you've got a tape, right, a tape where it looks like something bad might be happening?

SARAH: Yes.

LIZ: Then you take it to the fucking police. That way if something bad did happen, you won't get in trouble because you came forward, and if something bad didn't happen, you get a slap on the wrist and that's it. But if you don't take it to the cops, and something did happen and the cops find out about this tape and that you didn't bring it to them when you could have? That's when you could get into some actual serious real life grown up trouble and you don't want any part of that, okay?

SARAH: Okay.

LIZ: Okay. So, here's what gonna happen: you're gonna go home, get some sleep, and bring that thing over to the police station with your mom first thing in the morning. In the meantime, I and my associates will head over to Mike's thing so I can continue to watch Rob and Pete give my best friend alcohol poisoning. Okay? Okay.

APRIL: She's right, Sarah.

PETE: Yeah, that makes sense.

LUCY: Yeah.

LIZ: So we're good, then?

SARAH: I guess so.

LIZ: Good.

(The group starts getting their stuff together.)

ROB: And you guys don't...?

APRIL: What?

ROB: Nevermind.

APRIL: What is it?

ROB: Nothing, just. You guys don't think it's weird that we haven't heard anything about it? There's like, twelve people in this town and we've all got no life and great internet, you don't think it's weird that none of us have heard…?

LIZ: People can keep a secret when they need to.

ROB: Yeah, but what people, I mean, who was it?

SARAH: You mean who's on the tape?

LIZ: We don't need to know that.

PETE: Are any of us on the tape?

SARAH: I mean, we all are, at one point or another, but.

ROB: So, who was it?

APRIL: Who was what?

LIZ: We don't need to go there.

ROB: The girl. I'm just curious. I don't see what the harm is.

LIZ: I don't want to know who it was.

ROB: Why?

LIZ: For the same reason I don't want to see the tape.

ROB: And you don't think you're being a little over-dramatic?

PETE: I want to know, too.

LIZ: Well, I don't.

ROB: Then cover your ears. Who was the girl, Sarah?

PETE: Not the girl. I want to know who the guy is.

ROB: Why?

PETE: So I'll know who to kick the shit out of the next time I see him.

APRIL: Pete.

PETE: I'm serious.

LIZ: And this is why we shouldn't know who it was. We don't know what happened and yet all of a sudden…

ROB: Look, Sarah asked for our help and I think before we make any sort of a decision—

LIZ: We already made a decision. / She's bringing it to the cops.

ROB: You already made a decision.

PETE: Who was the guy, Sarah?

SARAH: Well, I don't know, I mean, now it seems complicated.

PETE: Complicated how?

SARAH: Well, like Liz said.

ROB: We just want to know who it was, I don't see how—

LIZ: And I'm saying we shouldn't know that and—

PETE: Well, how are we supposed to help Sarah make her decision unless—

SARAH: He's on the team. The guy, who. He's on the team and that's all I'm gonna say. Okay?

PETE: He's on the team?

LIZ: I don't want to know this.

SARAH: Yes.

PETE: On our team?

SARAH: Yes.

APRIL: And he isn't, like. He isn't in this room right now, is he?

SARAH: No.

APRIL: Well, good.

ROB: And thanks for the vote of confidence.

(APRIL *goes to sit with* DAISY.)

PETE: So, who was the girl?

LIZ: Pete.

ROB: It's okay, Sarah. We're gonna figure this out. I promise it won't get complicated. Now, who was the girl?

(*Beat*)

SARAH: Laura Heller.

PETE: Laura Heller?

APRIL: Sarah, Maggie, she's in your grade, right? Has she said anything about this? Should we call her? (*She gets her phone out.*)

LIZ: No. That is not what happens now. Sarah's gonna bring it to the cops and they're gonna call her. That's their job. And the rest of us, we are just going to forget that we were ever here and that we ever heard about any of this. That's our job. And now we are going to go, all right?

ROB: She's right.

LIZ: Thank you.

(APRIL *pockets her phone,* ROB *gets his coat.*)

ROB: She's totally right. I mean, obviously, we take it to the cops, right? I mean, obviously.

LIZ: Yes.

ROB: Yeah, I mean, if everything Liz is saying is right, then…

APRIL: Then what?

ROB: Well, nothing, just. Forget it. Don't even. Let's just go. Liz?

LIZ: Excellent idea. / Why didn't I think of it myself.

APRIL: No, wait. What is it?

LIZ: Guys.

APRIL: I want to know.

(ROB *stops.*)

ROB: Well, no, I just. I mean, I remember Laura that night, she was kinda… I mean, she's always kinda. Pete, back me up on this.

PETE: On what?

ROB: Well, no, I mean, nothing bad or anything, just, you know, it's Laura Heller. She's always been a little…

PETE: Obsessive?

ROB: Exactly.

APRIL: Obsessed with what?

PETE: Well.

ROB: With us.

APRIL: With you and Pete?

ROB: And Cal and Marshall and Wallace.

PETE: Mike Watts.

ROB: Mike Watts, Matt Lazarus.

PETE: Seth.

ROB: Seth Kannof and basically every other guy on the lacrosse team, and.

PETE: And we don't mean this in like, a bad way.

ROB: No, just that, look, she came to literally every lacrosse game last year, did you know that? I didn't even go to every lacrosse game last year and I'm on the lacrosse team.

APRIL: So did I.

ROB: Because you're our friend, you're friends with us, which she isn't. But she's always there and she's always, like, texting…

PETE: It's true, do you want to see how many messages I have from her?

APRIL: So, what's your point?

PETE: I'm still scrolling.

ROB: All I'm saying is if she ended up having sex with a guy on the team at that party I find it highly unlikely, that, I mean do you guys remember what she was wearing?

(The room reacts.)

APRIL: Are you serious?

ROB: Okay wait hang on, because, because okay, so look, so this is a picture of Laura at the party, okay? I'm on her profile, and this is a picture of what she was wearing, now that's not even, that's not even a dress, it's a skirt that happens to, it's a tank top, basically, and she's wearing it as a skirt.

APRIL: So?

ROB: So, I'm saying I'm thinking about how she was acting and I'm looking at what she was wearing and I think she came to this party with one thing in mind that makes what you guys are talking about / seem very unlikely.

LUCY: That's gross.

ROB: I'm just saying.

APRIL: Okay, but even if she did, whatever, and even if she came to the party wanting to get with one of the guys on the team.

ROB: Which, it's not like it would be the first time that that happened, either.

PETE: No.

APRIL: Well, fine, but you don't think it's weird that it happened like that, I mean, in public? You don't think that's a little weird? With everybody watching?

PETE: So, wait, so you think it's more likely that…?

ROB: Look, it was a weird night. I mean remember what Sarah got up to that night? And that was only what, ten thirty? And this is Sarah we're talking about.

SARAH: We could also not, actually?

MALCOLM: Wait, what happened?

APRIL: Nothing happened. We are not gonna talk about that.

LIZ: We shouldn't be talking about any of this.

ROB: She did a kind of a… what's the word?

PETE: A dance?

ROB: There was a kind of a dance that was done.

MALCOLM: A dance. / Like a…?

ROB: It was a sort of a…strip tease? / Is that the word?

SARAH: I don't remember this at all. I swear.

ROB: I do.

LUCY: I do, too, actually.

MALCOLM: Really?

LUCY: It was pretty rad, actually.

APRIL: Guys.

SARAH: You saw it?

LUCY: I got it.

PETE: It was a kind of a lapdance at points.

MALCOLM: Really?

SARAH: Did I get, I mean. I wasn't…?

LUCY: Strictly PG-13.

DAISY: Ish.

SARAH: How ish?

LUCY: You were there?

ROB: She's always there.

DAISY: Meaning what?

APRIL: Meaning, Sarah, that you tripped over your own shoelace trying to take your other sock off and Lucy and I put you to bed and locked the door around ten.

SARAH: How did we even get to talking about this?

ROB: Because this is exhibit B, okay? This is proof, in response to your question, that weird, public, sometimes even sexual sorta shit happens at parties like this all the time and it may seem weird now but in the context—

PETE: Totally normal.

ROB: Exactly. So, if Sarah Ferguson's gonna do a striptease at ten, who's to say Laura wasn't inspired to do something later? We don't know. Which is exactly why we don't take it to the cops.

LIZ: All right, look.

APRIL: Because stuff gets weird at parties and nothing happened? That's why we don't take it to the cops?

ROB: Exactly.

APRIL: Well, if stuff gets weird at parties but nothing happened, then why not take it to the cops? Wouldn't they know better than us if something was worth taking a look at?

PETE: No, they'll just fuck it up.

APRIL: What do you mean?

PETE: I mean, they'll just fuck it up. They'll hear rumors and see the tape and jump to conclusions. Look, did you hear about what happened to the teacher guy, over in Huntington?

MALCOLM: Who?

ROB: This was fucked up.

LIZ: True.

PETE: This girl goes around saying she slept with this teacher, he's like, twenty seven or something, she's sixteen, she says all these things, guy gets arrested, just based on a rumor, guy gets arrested, goes on trial where they find literally zero evidence against him, he doesn't go to prison or anything, but six months later he still can't get a job teaching because everybody thinks he did it, people are hounding him day and night, sending him death threats, and within six months this guy who's done nothing wrong, his life is so entirely fucked that he ties a belt around his neck, and.

APRIL: So, what's your point?

ROB: That Liz was wrong, there aren't two options. It's not if something happened or if something didn't happen there's also what if something didn't happen but we end up ruining some poor guy's life by getting him falsely accused of something he didn't do and can never get away from?

DAISY: So, how come she was unconscious?

(Beat. Everybody's watching now.)

DAISY: I mean, if she was so crazy about these guys that she was just desperate to have sex with any of them wherever whenever…I mean, if that's me, I'm not gonna need much in the way of alcohol.

ROB: Well, maybe she's not you. Maybe she's just a lightweight who drank too much and made a mistake?

PETE: And by the way, some people drink, you know, so that they can just let go and do whatever they want. Look, Daisy, everything else aside, do you really think a bunch of guys that we know would let something like that happen?

DAISY: I don't know what I think, do I think it's possible?

PETE: Yes.

DAISY: Yes.

PETE: Well, I don't.

DAISY: Why?

PETE: Because I know these guys, which you don't.

ROB: And we don't know for sure that she was unconscious, Sarah said she couldn't tell.

APRIL: So, you're saying, what, that she was "asking for it?"

ROB: Which, those are your words, by the way, not mine.

APRIL: But you're saying—

ROB: What I'm saying is, it was probably the best night of her life.

DAISY: And what about Sarah?

SARAH: What about Sarah?

DAISY: After you fell on your ass trying to take your top off, Lucy and April put you to bed and locked the door, right?

PETE: So?

DAISY: So, wasn't she "asking for it"?

ROB: No.

APRIL: So, Laura was "asking for it" but Sarah wasn't?

ROB: Sarah wasn't—

DAISY: She was taking her clothes off in the middle of her living room full of people that she invited over, are you honestly telling me that she wasn't -- I mean, what about Natalie, right now?

LIZ: Hey.

DAISY: What about Maggie, Liz? What if this was Maggie we were talking about and she was the one on that table—

LIZ: What about you shut your fucking / mouth for a second, Daisy?

DAISY: Would you still be so fucking worried about keeping out of it then?

ROB: No.

DAISY: No, what?

ROB: No, I would not look at Maggie in the same way. Or Natalie.

DAISY: Right, because you know them. You know Natalie. She's an actual living person to you that you care about, which Laura isn't. / She's just a groupie to you, right?

ROB: No, because she's not, that isn't.

DAISY: (Re: NATALIE) And Christ, look at what she's wearing, Rob. / What does that mean, huh? How come she didn't wear a fucking turtleneck if she didn't want to get—

LIZ: Can you stop?

APRIL: What is the difference, Rob? Between Laura and Natalie or Sarah that night? What's the difference?

ROB: You guys keep trying to make me the bad guy, here, but.

APRIL: What's the difference?

ROB: The way she was acting. The way she was -- Her intention.

PETE: Look, can I just—

ROB: Take it away.

(APRIL *and* DAISY *share a moment; they make a good team.*)

PETE: I mean, it's Laura Heller. Does anybody in this room really believe that Laura Heller would keep something like this to herself? Am I the only one who remembers how in middle school she used to cut her own wrists with like a whatever a butter knife just so she could get the attention from everybody?

DAISY: Jesus.

ROB: It's true.

PETE: Look, I don't have anything against Laura Heller. I don't want anything bad to happen to her. I don't want anything bad to happen to anyone. I just don't think it did. And I believe that if she got hurt like we hope she didn't, she would have told somebody.

LIZ: Pete, you know I love you, right?

PETE: Yeah, why?

LIZ: Because you really don't know what in the fuck what you're talking about.

ROB: You don't think she would have said anything?

SARAH: Well, actually, she probably wouldn't even have had to.

ROB: Had to what?

SARAH: Tell anybody. I mean, when you get attacked, you've gotta go to the hospital, there's all this stuff, that, and if she did go to the hospital like she woulda had to…

APRIL: Wait a second, Sarah, did he…?

SARAH: Did he what?

APRIL: On the tape, can you see…I don't know, did you see…what happened? Did he…?

(APRIL *looks to* DAISY.)

DAISY: Did he finish in her? / Right?

ROB: Jesus.

(*The room shifts, uncomfortably.*)

DAISY: Look, if we're gonna talk about it, let's talk about it. Was he wearing a condom? Did he pull out?

SARAH: I don't know, the tape cut off while it was still, um.

DAISY: So you couldn't see—

ROB: She just said that you couldn't see.

DAISY: Were they laying down?

ROB: Jesus, Daisy.

DAISY: Were they laying down? On the table?

ROB: Why does it matter?

SARAH: He was standing. She was laying down.

ROB: What does this matter?

PETE: It doesn't matter. But your point was, Sarah, that if something did happen to her, she would have had to have gone to the doctor, at which point that doctor would have had to have called the police because she's a minor at which point the police would have swarmed the school, right?

ROB: Which they haven't, ergo, nothing happened.

NATALIE: You don't have to go to the hospital.

(*Beat. Everyone's looking right at* NATALIE.)

NATALIE: What?

DAISY: You were saying something?

NATALIE: I, uh.

PETE: Does she need to lie down?

APRIL: Natalie? What were you going to say?

NATALIE: Well, I knew a girl this one time who was coming home one night and it was late and she'd never been to the bar before and she was younger than they were, so her friends insisted she took a cab home because they wanted her to be safe, and so she got to her door and the cab drove away, and at some point in between opening the door and closing the door and the cab driving away, while she was getting the key in the mail thing. *(Beat)* Anyway, she had this thing happen, where, you know there's this wall on the inside it's a very important wall and from what I'm told, it just hurts like hell when somebody rips a hole right through it, there's blood everywhere. *(Beat)* But you know, you don't have to go to the hospital right away if you don't want to. You just got the shit kicked out of you. You don't have to do anything if you don't want to. If you want, you can just sit there. Bleed for a bit, if you're bleeding. Or if you want you can go to the hospital and you can give a fake name or a fake insurance and then when they're not looking, you can go, but, you don't have to go right away. Not if you don't want to. *(Beat)* She hasn't even told her mom yet.

PETE: Why would you use a fake name?

NATALIE: Hm?

MALCOLM: Because, you're like, embarrassed, right?

ROB: Why would you be embarrassed?

NATALIE: That's a very good question.

(Beat)

LUCY: Maybe we should take a vote.

APRIL: That's a good idea.

MALCOLM: Like a preliminary?

LUCY: Just to see where we are. Numbers wise. Nothing final.

LIZ: We're voting on this now?

ROB: Sarah asked for our help.

APRIL: That's a good idea.

ROB: Sure, yeah.

PETE: Works for me.

ROB: Liz?

LIZ: Yeah, this'll end well.

SARAH: Okay. I guess I'll, uh. All in favor of—

APRIL: Maybe we should like, close our eyes? Maybe?

ROB: I wanna see where people stand.

PETE: Me, too.

APRIL: Yeah, but I think people might have an easier time being honest if they don't have to—

DAISY: She's right.

ROB: Fine. We'll close our eyes.

SARAH: Okay, you ready? I'll do yes, no, or abstention. Okay? Okay. Everybody close your eyes. All in favor of taking it to the cops?

(APRIL, DAISY, LIZ, LUCY, MALCOLM, and NATALIE all raise their hands.)

SARAH: All opposed?

(PETE, ROB, and, after a moment, MAGGIE raise their hands.)

SARAH: Um. Abstentions? (She raises her hand.) Okay, it's, uh. Six to three in favor of taking it to the cops. And one abstention.

PETE: So, who was the third? On our side?

APRIL: I'm not sure you're fully grasping the purpose of a secret ballot process.

ROB: Which was put in place so people would tell the truth, which, they've already done that, and now I wanna…

PETE: Liz?

LIZ: I voted yes.

PETE: Really?

DAISY: It's okay. Everybody gets to vote however they want.

ROB: *(Re:* NATALIE*)* What about this one?

SARAH: She voted yes, too.

DAISY: Don't look at me.

APRIL: Or me.

LUCY: I'm with them.

MALCOLM: Yeah, me too.

SARAH: I abstained.

ROB: So, wait, so that means.

PETE: No. Fucking. Way.

(They all turn to see MAGGIE, *who does her best to look casual.)*

LIZ: Maggie?

MAGGIE: It's just what I / voted, okay?

LIZ: Maggie, I don't understand.

ROB: It's okay. She gets to vote however she wants, right, Daisy?

LIZ: Maggie, you're in class with Laura. She's been to our house.

ROB: She doesn't have to explain herself.

MAGGIE: I just don't want to say, okay? I thought we said—

LIZ: Why not? Why don't you want to say?

APRIL: Maggie.

LIZ: Would you let me handle this, please?

MAGGIE: Because you aren't gonna get it.

LIZ: Get what?

ROB: She doesn't have to / explain herself.

MAGGIE: You won't understand.

(LIZ *kneels down in front of her sister.*)

LIZ: Then explain it to me. Please. I'll listen. I promise. Just. What's going on?

(*Beat. Everyone's watching her.*)

MAGGIE: Look, do you guys really think she doesn't know? She knows. What she is to you. She's smarter than anybody else in here by half. Do you really think she doesn't know she's a joke to you?

LIZ: Maggie.

MAGGIE: She knows that, she's always known that, and she comes anyway. To your games, to your parties.

DAISY: Maggie, were you in the room with Laura Heller? When this happened?

MAGGIE: Lizzie.

LIZ: Answer her question, please.

(*Beat*)

MAGGIE: It was late. / Most everybody else was gone already.

LIZ: Fucking shit.

MAGGIE: The lights were mostly off but there was this Christmas tree with red and green lights across the way that—

DAISY: And how many of you were there?

MAGGIE: Six or seven, probably. There was music coming in from the other room so it was soft.

APRIL: And where was Laura?

MAGGIE: They were leaning up against the island, at first, the table you have in the middle of your kitchen, Sarah? And it was strange, I wasn't used to seeing her like that.

DAISY: Like what?

MAGGIE: Happy. *(Beat)* She looked so happy. She was so close to him. He had his hand on her arm. We had all split up. Two by two. And every time I looked over, it was a little different. At first, he's making jokes into her ear and she's smiling into her lap and then he's kissing her, you know. He's kissing her.

APRIL: And what happened next?

MAGGIE: He was holding her.

DAISY: And?

MAGGIE: Nobody holds Laura Heller like that. Not ever. Look, you don't know her, but I know her. And watching her like that, it just made me so… happy. We all were. We were together and we started watching and they didn't seem to care, so. It was strange, like, I knew it was strange, but it didn't feel strange, you know? People were smiling, laughing, cheering, even. It was.

DAISY: Cheering?

MAGGIE: You know, joke stuff. Egging them on. Telling them to do stuff. But they didn't even notice, so.

APRIL: And then what?

MAGGIE: I mean, I didn't know that sorta stuff really happened, I mean, not in public, like, I'd never seen anything like that before except like, on the internet but after what happened with Sarah, it didn't seem so strange, you know? I mean, I was embarrassed at first, but that was only because I didn't get what it was yet.

APRIL: And what was it?

MAGGIE: Beautiful. Look, I know what it must look like just to see it on a tape, but in reality it wasn't like what you guys think it is. It wasn't violent or scary it was this girl being kissed and loved who never gets kissed or loved and I think Rob was right, you know? I think it might just have been the best night of her life.

APRIL: And what makes you say that?

MAGGIE: Because it was the best night of mine.

DAISY: Were her eyes open?

(Beat)

MAGGIE: What do you mean?

DAISY: Her eyes. Were they open?

MAGGIE: I mean they were kissing, and.

DAISY: Was she moving?

MAGGIE: Moving what?

APRIL: Maggie, come on.

MAGGIE: Moving what?

DAISY: Anything. An arm, a leg.

MAGGIE: When?

DAISY: When he pulled his pants down and -- Were her eyes open? Was she moving? Could she move?

MAGGIE: I don't— / Lizzie?

APRIL: Sarah said she looked unconscious, Maggie. Was she? This is very important.

MAGGIE: I don't, I can't remember.

DAISY: You don't remember if her eyes were open.

MAGGIE: No.

DAISY: The Christmas tree lights from across the street you remember, the music you remember. / You remember everything except the answers to our questions.

MAGGIE: It was late, I was drunk. It was dark. We all were. / Lizzie, please.

DAISY: We need to know if she was moving.

MAGGIE: It wasn't what you think. It wasn't like that. It couldn't have been. / We wouldn't have let something happen like that.

DAISY: And what if you were wrong? What if you didn't know what you were looking at? What if she was unconscious and he was on top of her while you cheered him on?

MAGGIE: That's not what happened.

DAISY: Yeah, and how in the fuck would you know?

MAGGIE: I was there. I remember.

DAISY: You don't remember shit. You don't remember if her eyes were open. You can't remember if she moved or not.

MAGGIE: No, I can remember. I can. And I know that it wasn't what you think it was.

(DAISY *gets an idea.*)

DAISY: Really?

MAGGIE: Yes.

DAISY: You can remember?

MAGGIE: Yes.

LIZ: Daisy.

DAISY: Okay, so, who undid his belt?

MAGGIE: What do you mean?

DAISY: I thought you said you remembered?

MAGGIE: I do.

DAISY: So who undid his belt? Did he do it or did she do it?

MAGGIE: He did.

DAISY: And who undid his shirt?

MAGGIE: He did.

DAISY: And her shirt?

MAGGIE: Well.

DAISY: And her dress?

MAGGIE: Liz?

DAISY: Were her hands on his face, Maggie? This guy that she's been waiting for so long to be loved by, to be kissed by? Did she kiss him back? Was she moving at all?

MAGGIE: Lizzie.

DAISY: Who undid his belt, Maggie?

MAGGIE: Lizzie? *(Beat)* But, but don't sometimes, when people kiss, don't they close their eyes?

(Nobody says anything.)

APRIL: Were Laura's eyes open. Was she moving.

MAGGIE: No.

DAISY: Okay, then. That's it. *(She heads for SARAH.)*

MAGGIE: Wait.

DAISY: We're done here. / Time to bring it to the cops.

MAGGIE: I don't understand.

ROB: *(He gets in Daisy's way)* All right, / hang on.

MAGGIE: I don't understand.

DAISY: No, it's done. There isn't any question anymore.
She was unconscious. That was what Sarah didn't
know and now we know.

APRIL: She's right.

DAISY: Now, gimme the tape, Sarah.

ROB: Sarah, do not give her that tape.

DAISY: You asked us for our help. You said you wanted
to do the right thing, didn't you?

SARAH: Yes.

DAISY: Then give me the tape.

ROB: We haven't even made / a decision yet.

DAISY: You guys need more evidence? Great. Let's
bring it to the cops and I'm sure they'll find us some.

PETE: There's a lot on the line, here, Daisy, we just want
to be sure before we risk / turning somebody's life
upside down.

MAGGIE: Lizzie…?

DAISY: Just gimme the tape, Sarah. Give it to me and it
won't be on your shoulders anymore.

ROB: And Sarah brought it to all of us.

DAISY: So?

MAGGIE: Lizzie, please, Lizzie.

ROB: So I think we should all have to agree.

DAISY: Well what is it gonna take for us all to agree?

MAGGIE: Lizzie, please.

DAISY: What is it going to take?

MAGGIE: Lizzie?

LIZ: *(Wheeling on her)* Maggie, you say my name one more time and I swear to Christ I'm gonna put you through a fucking wall do you understand me?

(Beat. MAGGIE *nods. Everybody's watching.)*

LIZ: We're not releasing it.

DAISY: Excuse me?

LIZ: We aren't having this discussion anymore, Daisy. April, please, don't fight me on this. We aren't releasing that tape. Now, / this thing happened…

DAISY: Oh, really.

LIZ: This thing happened and now it's over and it's too late for us to do anything about it, too late for the cops to do anything about it, run any tests. It's been six weeks.

DAISY: A girl got / raped, Liz, do you not—

LIZ: And guess what? I can't fix that. I can't fix that. If I could, I would. But releasing that tape won't change what happened. All it's gonna do—

DAISY: That's bullshit.

APRIL: Liz, not twenty minutes ago you looked at / Sarah and you said—

LIZ: And I was wrong, then. I was wrong.

APRIL: Because you didn't know Maggie was there?

LIZ: Because it isn't going to do anything. It isn't going to help anybody. All it's gonna do is hurt the wrong people and I'm not / gonna let that happen.

DAISY: Hurt the wrong people, like who, like Maggie? You aren't worried about Laura, obviously.

LIZ: Like Maggie, yes, and every other kid on that tape. Every other moron like my sister, who was in that room, they are gonna show that tape over and over and over again and then they're gonna come after the rest of the people who are on that tape, which is every single one of us, I mean, Sarah said so.

DAISY: This isn't about us.

LIZ: They're gonna make it about us.

DAISY: How?

LIZ: Because they're gonna put your face on T V next to the video and a big fucking sign that says "HIGH SCHOOL RAPE PARTIES IN CRAIGSTOWN, INDIANA."

MAGGIE: That isn't what happened.

LIZ: Yes. It. Is. *(Beat)* It just doesn't matter. We're not releasing the tape.

APRIL: Oh, come on.

LIZ: We bring this thing to the cops, and the next day, people get arrested, the tape gets leaked, because of course it will, and now it's online. Now it's on the internet, the news trucks start arriving, now they're on our lawns, in our school, in our face. The town is in fucking chaos and—

APRIL: Why would they want to talk to us?

LIZ: Because the minute this thing drops, Laura, and whoever the guy is, they go into hiding, but the reporters still need their story and that means anybody who was on the tape. They're gonna put our faces, drunk, laughing, they're gonna put it right up on T V and that's how they'll know us. The rest of the world. Colleges. That's how Northwestern is gonna see Natalie and everything she worked for, everything she and her mom worked for is gonna / get completely—

APRIL: You don't know that. / You don't know that, Liz.

LIZ: Do you really think they're gonna let you into their school, Natalie? And with all that scholarship money?

(NATALIE *looks away.*)

APRIL: You don't know that.

LIZ: Of course I do. They are gonna ruin the lives of the people who were on that tape. Who were at that party.

APRIL: Why?

LIZ: Because it'll make great T V.

DAISY: And?

LIZ: And Laura Heller still got—hurt. We can't change that. No matter what happens, from this point on, if we release this thing the only people that are gonna get hurt are you and me and us. Anything we wanted out of our lives—

DAISY: That's not good enough.

ROB: Well, not for you, maybe. But why would it be?

APRIL: Rob.

ROB: No, true or false, Daisy, this time next year you're gonna be working at the Dunkin Donuts / on route nine anyway so what do you care if—

APRIL: Don't you talk to her like that. / Don't you dare talk to her like that.

PETE: Do we all want to take a breather, here?

ROB: Like what?

APRIL: Like you're better than her.

LUCY: Guys.

LIZ: This is all beside the point.

APRIL: So what is the point?

LIZ: If you release this tape, all that's gonna happen is you're gonna hurt the wrong people, and I will not let this moron throw her life away.

DAISY: Not for Laura Heller?

LIZ: We can't change what happened. All we can do now is damage control, we can deal with this in our own way, see to her in our own way, / we can make sure—

APRIL: "Damage control?"

(Beat)

LIZ: April.

APRIL: I'm sorry, but did you really just call what / happened to Laura…?

LIZ: April, do you really think that—

APRIL: She's fifteen years old. They stripped her naked and put her on a table and you look at me right now. Look at me, Liz. Look at me. She could be scared. It was six weeks ago? She didn't go the hospital? She could be pregnant. Or sick. And scared and alone. She's alone, Liz. How can you do this?

LIZ: She's my sister. I don't have a choice.

APRIL: Yeah, and neither did Laura Heller. But I do have a choice, and I'm gonna do what we should have done an hour ago. I'm gonna call her. *(She gets her phone out.)*

LIZ: April.

APRIL: No, I need to hear it from her.

ROB: April, you don't want to do that.

LIZ: April, just stop. Just think for a second and wait.

APRIL: Wait for what?

ROB: For us to decide.

APRIL: And who said we get to decide?

ROB: Sarah did, the second she told us about it, and now—

APRIL: She's been living with this for six weeks.

ROB: And we've had it for less than an hour.

PETE: Okay, maybe we should all / just calm down.

APRIL: No, I need to talk to her, I need to talk to her and make sure that she's okay. / I need to…

ROB: April.

DAISY: Leave her alone.

ROB: April, you call her right now and you are only gonna make this thing ten times more complicated. / You're gonna turn this whole thing into…

APRIL: I need to know if she's okay. / That is the only thing that matters.

ROB: April, you do this and you'll regret it.

DAISY: Was that a threat?

ROB: This isn't what you think it was.

APRIL: So, what was it, then?

ROB: You just need to trust me on this.

APRIL: And I need a reason.

ROB: You just / have to trust me.

APRIL: That's not good enough.

ROB: April.

APRIL: I'm calling her.

LIZ: Put the phone down, April.

DAISY: Back off.

LIZ: Will somebody get this / bitch out of my face, please?

ROB: April, please. You don't want to do this.

APRIL: Why?

ROB: Because it's Cal.

(*Beat*)

(*O S. Laura's voice, filtered "Hello? Hello? Is anybody—".*)

(APRIL *hangs up. Beat*)

ROB: I told you, didn't I? Didn't I tell you? I told you to just trust me. If you'd just trusted me, that's.

LIZ: You were there?

DAISY: Tell me you're surprised by this.

SARAH: You weren't. / I never saw you there.

ROB: Listen to me, everybody listen to me right now.

SARAH: I didn't see you in the tape.

LIZ: You were there?

ROB: Listen, I never lied to you.

PETE: Robbie? (*His face is a mask of disbelief and horror.*)

ROB: Look, I was drunk. We all were. But it wasn't—

PETE: Was she unconscious?

ROB: Pete. / It wasn't what you think.

SARAH: I didn't see you in the room.

LIZ: What are you talking about?

PETE: Was she unconscious?

ROB: Pete.

PETE: Was she?

ROB: It was like what Maggie said, okay? People started getting sloppy. Everybody was making out, Cal and Laura just took it further than the rest of us. It's not like he's some guy in an alley. Cal wouldn't do that. And I didn't lie about anything. I just wanted to keep his name out of it in case stuff got you know…

PETE: Sloppy? (*He can't believe what he's hearing.*)

ROB: Yes. Yes, exactly. But I never lied to you. I was gonna tell you the second we left, all of it, I swear. I just didn't think it was important. You get that, right?

DAISY: Wait, so, which was it?

ROB: What do you mean?

DAISY: Were you gonna tell him after or did you not think it was important?

ROB: You want to stay out of this, please?

DAISY: And after you made us sit through all that bullshit about what clothes she was wearing, if she wanted it, you / pathetic—

ROB: Listen, would you just listen?

SARAH: You're not on the tape.

ROB: What?

DAISY: What are you talking about?

SARAH: You aren't on the tape, Rob, how are you not on the tape?

ROB: What does it matter whether—

SARAH: Oh. Right.

APRIL: What?

SARAH: You filmed it. Right?

LIZ: You filmed it?

ROB: I mean.

LIZ: Idiot.

PETE: Robbie.

DAISY: You don't disappoint, Rob, / I'll give you that.

ROB: Would you shut up?

LIZ: You stupid fucking idiot child / do you understand what you've done?

ROB: Liz.

PETE: Why would you film it?

ROB: I thought it'd be funny. *(Beat)* I mean, Cal Summers and Laura Heller? I thought. *(Beat)* Look, it was mistake. It's Cal, you guys. I'm serious, now. He's our friend. Do you really think he'd do something like—

DAISY: This is pathetic.

ROB: *(Getting worked up, a little desperate)* It was a mistake. He's just a kid. The night was crazy but he's just a kid, like we all are, he's got his whole life ahead of him, and. Do you guys really believe that he deserves to have his whole life thrown away? Because of one night? One mistake, with a girl who was crazy about him anyway? Because of one thing that he did one night when he was seventeen, his whole life is gonna be... It was just a mistake, what, has nobody ever made a mistake, before? No, no. He is my friend. He is my friend, and I am not gonna—

APRIL: Shut up.

ROB: April.

APRIL: Just shut up.

ROB: April, please.

DAISY: She said—

APRIL: He's right.

(Beat)

DAISY: April?

APRIL: There has to be something we don't know.

DAISY: What are you / talking about?

APRIL: Cal wouldn't do this. I'm sorry, Daisy, but he wouldn't. There's just no way.

DAISY: He was drunk.

APRIL: Yeah, well I've seen Cal drunk. He isn't like that.

PETE: He can be.

APRIL: Not with me.

DAISY: He wasn't with you.

APRIL: He wouldn't do this.

DAISY: You don't know that.

APRIL: I know him.

DAISY: April.

APRIL: It's Cal. He does the musical, for God's sake, and do you have any idea, Daisy, look at me, do you have any idea how many times he's driven me home late at night and / there has to be something…

DAISY: I can't believe I'm hearing this.

APRIL: And last summer by the lake when we were all drunk, I was gone, and we went for a walk all alone and if he wanted to. But he didn't. He didn't because he wouldn't. Not ever.

DAISY: April.

APRIL: No, there's gotta be something else that we don't know. Maggie and Rob said they were flirting, maybe? Maybe they talked about it before. Maybe she wanted to, and.

DAISY: April, listen to me.

APRIL: He wouldn't hurt anyone.

DAISY: You don't know that.

APRIL: I know him. He's my friend.

DAISY: And if it was me?

APRIL: If it was you then I would stand by you, too, I wouldn't believe what anyone said no matter how—

DAISY: I mean if it was me instead of Laura.

APRIL: That isn't—

ROB: He just made a mistake. They both did.

DAISY: And who's to say he won't make it again?

APRIL: He won't. / He wouldn't.

DAISY: You don't know that. You don't know that.

APRIL: Daisy, I know Cal like you know me.

DAISY: I don't know you.

(*This hits* APRIL *like a shot. Beat*)

NATALIE: Okay, what if we just wait?

MALCOLM: Wait for what?

ROB: Hang on. Have you been here this whole time?

MALCOLM: Well.

ROB: I'm serious, you talk / like, once an hour, and.

APRIL: Wait for what, Natalie?

(MALCOLM *just looks away, fumes.*)

NATALIE: To get out of this place. Get into schools. Get our scholarships set up, and once we're all set…?

DAISY: Liz really got to you, didn't she?

NATALIE: What if we just wait? Could we just… wait? I mean, is it time sensitive? Will that… Could we do that?

ROB: If we wait, they'll just ask Sarah why she kept it hidden so long.

NATALIE: She could say she only just found it.

ROB: Which they'll believe then about as much as I believe her now. We need to make a decision. Tonight.

NATALIE: Drink.

(NATALIE *takes her flask out and starts drinking again.* LIZ *just looks away.*)

SARAH: Maybe we should vote again? Might be good to see where we're at, plus, I think we could all do with a few seconds of not talking.

PETE: Yeah, okay.

APRIL: Eyes closed?

DAISY: Our eyes should be open this time.

APRIL: Why?

DAISY: Because our eyes should be open this time.

APRIL: Fine.

SARAH: All in favor of bringing the tape to the cops?

(DAISY, LUCY, *and* MALCOLM *raise their hands.*)

SARAH: All opposed?

(APRIL, LIZ, MAGGIE, NATALIE, PETE, *and* ROB *raise their hands.*)

ROB: Time to pick a side, Sarah.

(SARAH *raises her hand.*)

SARAH: Seven to three.

DAISY: Well, that wasn't so hard, was it?

NATALIE: I wanna go home.

ROB: We're almost there.

LUCY: You know, there is one person who we haven't heard from yet, and it's sorta the only person that matters.

APRIL: Cal?

LUCY: Laura. I mean, maybe we should call her again. Ask her this time.

ROB: So, you'd put this on her?

LUCY: Not put it on her. Give her the option. Let her decide.

DAISY: That's a good idea.

ROB: I disagree.

DAISY: Why, I'm shocked, Rob.

ROB: Well, what if she thinks she can get something out of it?

DAISY: Out of what?

ROB: Out of it looking like she was, you know, you remember what Pete said about the butter knife? What if we present her with the opportunity and even if nothing happened she might...

MAGGIE: Laura wouldn't do that. / She's not like that.

DAISY: We know what happened, even Liz said it.

APRIL: She's wrong.

DAISY: Then why don't we watch the tape, then?

APRIL: What?

DAISY: You all don't mind talking about her and saying shit about her and deciding what happens to her for her but heaven forbid you should actually have to watch while your friend—

APRIL: Cal Summers didn't—

DAISY: Then why don't you call him, April? Why don't you call him and then when he says something you don't like, you can hang up on him, too.

APRIL: Daisy.

DAISY: Why don't you call him?

ROB: Well, what about Laura?

DAISY: What about Laura?

ROB: I mean, it's been six weeks. If she hasn't said anything, which she hasn't, isn't that her telling us what she wants? By not saying anything? Maybe she doesn't want people knowing. And who are we to decide what she needs?

DAISY: Are you serious?

LIZ: He isn't wrong, you know, and however bad the whatever, the media stuff would be? For us? Can you imagine how much worse it would be for her? I mean, this would define her entire life, whatever happened. People would make sure of it. That's what her whole life would be about. People would be calling her house, she'd get death threats.

ROB: And in the end, I wouldn't be surprised if she ends up cutting her wrists with something a hell of a lot sharper than a butter knife.

MALCOLM: Yeah, that's some bullshit, Rob.

(*Everybody looks to* MALCOLM.)

ROB: I'm sorry?

MALCOLM: Sorry, but that's just some bullshit, right there.

ROB: What are you talking about?

MALCOLM: She was asleep.

ROB: So?

MALCOLM: She was asleep. And I'll grant you that things get confusing sometimes, especially when you're drinking—

ROB: Which they both were.

MALCOLM: So?

ROB: So why are we holding him to a higher standard when they were both drunk and they both made a mistake?

MALCOLM: Because it was different.

ROB: How?

MALCOLM: Because he could stand.

LUCY: Mal.

ROB: All right, look—

MALCOLM: So don't say it was for her, okay? It's a lie. You're lying. Even Pete knows that.

ROB: Shut up.

MALCOLM: No, I won't shut up. This is wrong. It's just black and white and it's wrong.

LIZ: Says the only guy who wasn't at the party.

MALCOLM: Meaning what?

LIZ: Meaning you've got a shit-ton less to lose than the rest of us.

ROB: Oh, I wouldn't say that.

MALCOLM: No, she's right. I wasn't there. I don't even know what I'm doing here now, but you know something, Rob? I'm glad I am. I mean it. I am so glad that / after all of the fucking time of feeling like shit—

ROB: What are you even / talking about?

MALCOLM: Because I didn't get to go to your stupid parties, because I knew you would make my life a living hell, I am just so glad that I am here so I can see you for what you really are, and you know something? It makes me sick. All of you. *(Beat. Fuck it)* I love her, did you know that? Did you even know that we're in love and we've been together for a fucking year, and do you know why you didn't know that? Why none of you know that? Because I told her not to tell you. I

begged her. Because I was afraid of you, Rob. Afraid of
what you'd say to her. What you'd do to her. But I'm
not afraid of you anymore.

LUCY: Mal.

MALCOLM: I see you for what you are and you can't
control me anymore. I didn't do anything wrong. I
wasn't there because I'm not your friend and I wasn't
at your party so I'm not on that fucking tape.

ROB: She is.

(ROB's *pointing right at* LUCY. MALCOLM *doesn't buy it for
a second.*)

MALCOLM: (*"Yeah right"*) Fuck you.

ROB: Fine.

MALCOLM: No, she isn't.

ROB: Okay, fine.

LUCY: Mal.

MALCOLM: No, she isn't.

APRIL: Lucy?

LUCY: Malcolm.

MALCOLM: No, she isn't. There's no way.

ROB: Gimme the tape, Sarah.

LIZ: I thought we said?

ROB: You want me to end this? You want this done?
You want this out of your life, forever? Give me the
fucking tape.

LIZ: Sarah, don't.

SARAH: We shouldn't—

ROB: Then ask her, then. Ask Lucy if she was there. Ask
her if she was any better than me.

LUCY: Rob, just stop it, okay? Just stop.

MALCOLM: You're full of shit.

ROB: You weren't there. How the hell would you know?

MALCOLM: Because I know her.

ROB: Then, ask her.

MALCOLM: No.

ROB: Then, what are you so afraid of?

MALCOLM: Fine. Lucy…?

(Beat. LUCY doesn't say no.)

MALCOLM: Lucy?

LUCY: Look, can we talk about this outside?

MALCOLM: I don't understand. / You were there?

LUCY: Look, I'm—can we talk about this outside, please?

MALCOLM: You were there?

LUCY: Mal.

MALCOLM: And you didn't tell me?

ROB: Man. Wonder what else she hasn't told you.

(And suddenly, MALCOLM takes a swing at ROB. They wrestle, struggle, until the group splits them up.)

MALCOLM: Lemme go.

ROB: Please, no, please, let him. Come on.

MALCOLM: Let me GO.

(PETE puts ROB into a wall and pins him there, anger coursing through him. Beat. After a moment, PETE lets go and walks away.)

ROB: *(To MALCOLM)* You are so full of shit.

LUCY: Mal.

ROB: Psycho.

NATALIE: I wanna go home.

LUCY: Mal.

(*Beat.* MALCOLM *doesn't say anything. Nobody does.*)

ROB: All in favor?

(DAISY *raises her hand. She's the only one.*)

ROB: All opposed?

(APRIL, LIZ, LUCY, MAGGIE, NATALIE, PETE, ROB, SARAH, *and, with a look at* LUCY, MALCOLM—*all raise their hand.* LIZ *looks* DAISY *right in the eye.*)

LIZ: Well, okay then.

(*Beat. Everybody braces for the inevitable showdown. And then:*)

LIZ: We're done here. (*She goes to get her stuff together.*)

ROB: Exactly. Wait, what?

LIZ: It's done. Maggie, get your stuff.

(LIZ *gets her coat on. Nobody else moves.*)

ROB: What are you talking about / it's done.

LIZ: Daisy isn't going to say anything, Rob. It's over. We all agreed.

DAISY: Really?

LIZ: Daisy isn't going to say anything.

DAISY: Like hell I'm not.

LIZ: No, you're not, Daisy. You wouldn't do that.

PETE: Did I miss something?

DAISY: You think I give a shit what happens to you or your sister?

LIZ: No, I meant you wouldn't do that to April. / April, who sticks up for you. April, who'd do anything for you.

DAISY: April doesn't have anything to do with this. April wasn't there. April wasn't even in the room.

LIZ: Then let me ask you this, Daisy, which story do you think people are gonna find more surprising? That some dumbass idiot frat boy jock raped a girl at a party in the middle of nowhere, Indiana? Or that six weeks later, ten of his very best friends got together in the middle of the night to keep it a secret? *(Beat)* This isn't about Cal or Laura Heller anymore. We are the story now. And if you release this tape, April will be the face of it. Sarah called April first. April unlocked the door to let us in when she wasn't supposed to. None of this could have happened without April to say nothing of the fact that she's in love with him.

APRIL: Liz.

LIZ: Truly, madly, adorably in love with the boy on that tape, hurting that girl. April, who not five minutes ago voted to keep it a secret anyway?

APRIL: That's not what happened.

LIZ: It doesn't matter what happened. It matters what it looks like. Now, you answer me, Daisy: how does this look for April, if you release this tape?

DAISY: You really are a fucking lunatic, you know that?

LIZ: No, I'm not. This is just what I'm willing to do for my sister. Now, what are you willing to do for yours?

(Beat)

DAISY: April, you gotta say something, here.

APRIL: I'm sorry.

DAISY: April, please.

APRIL: I'm sorry, but I don't believe…

DAISY: You can't let it end like this.

LIZ: I'm sorry about this, Daisy. I really am. I know how much you were / looking forward to being a hero in all this.

DAISY: Would you shut the fuck up. April. Please.

(APRIL *looks away. She's not gonna say anything.*)

LIZ: So, what's it gonna be?

ROB: All in favor?

(*Nobody raises their hands.*)

ROB: All opposed?

(APRIL, LIZ, LUCY, MAGGIE, MALCOLM, NATALIE, PETE, ROB, *and* SARAH, *all raise their hands, and finally,* DAISY *does, too.*)

ROB: May I?

(SARAH *hands* ROB *the camera, who stuffs it quietly into his bag and zips it shut.*)

ROB: Okay.

APRIL: I'm gonna start locking up.

(*Over the following,* APRIL *switches on the ghost light and returns it to its original position.* SARAH *looks around at her friends.*)

SARAH: I'm so sorry about all of this, I, I just, I didn't know what to do, and.

PETE: Of course you did.

SARAH: Pete.

PETE: Of course you did. If you didn't know what it was, if you thought it was nothing, you would have just deleted it. You knew exactly what it was. And you knew what you had to do, you were just too scared to do it. You came here so we could tell you what to do and now we have.

SARAH: I didn't want anybody to get hurt.

LIZ: Yeah? And how'd that work out for you?

MALCOLM: I gotta get out of here.

(MALCOLM *tosses his coat on and heads for the door*, LUCY *following. From off stage, by the door, we hear:*)

LUCY: Mal. Malcolm. Please, wait.

MALCOLM: I gotta get out of here, okay? Just.

LUCY: I'm sorry, okay? It was late and it was scary and Maggie and I, we were the only girls in the room and she was gone, you know? What was I supposed to do?

MALCOLM: Just stop it, all right?

LUCY: *(Near tears)* What was I supposed to do, Malcolm? I was the only other girl in the room, what was I supposed to…?

MALCOLM: Shut up, please, just shut up…

LUCY: What was I supposed to…

(MALCOLM *exits, slamming the door in* LUCY's *face*. APRIL *exits backstage and* NATALIE *stumbles, falls to the ground. She doesn't look so good. Her flask is empty.*)

PETE: We should get her home.

ROB: You need any help with that?

PETE: No.

ROB: Pete.

LIZ: Maggie?

MAGGIE: I think I'm gonna stay with Sarah, tonight. I already told mom I was, so.

LIZ: Well, yeah, but.

MAGGIE: I'm gonna go with Sarah.

LIZ: Maggie.

(MAGGIE *recoils from her. Like she's frightened of her.*)

MAGGIE: I'll see you tomorrow, Liz.

LIZ: Maggie?

(MAGGIE *goes to exit.*)

SARAH: I'm sorry, you guys. I'm so sorry.

(SARAH *follows, and after a moment, they're gone.*)

PETE: Come on, Liz. We should get her home.

LIZ: Yeah, okay. I'll give you a lift after we drop off this one.

(LIZ *gets under* NATALIE's *other arm, and they head for the exit.*)

ROB: I'll see you guys on Monday, yeah?

NATALIE: Hey, did you guys hear? I got into college.

LIZ: That's wonderful, baby.

(*And they exit.* ROB *is alone.* LUCY, *crushed, returns to her bag where she finds her keys, her phone, and the whiskey bottle that she never got to give to* MALCOLM, *and is rocked.* ROB *goes to her:*)

ROB: Hey, listen to me, okay? They're gonna come around. You know that, right? Malcolm, too. They're gonna come around. People just need to blow off some steam, but I'll tell you something else—

LUCY: You shouldn't have said what you said.

ROB: Look.

LUCY: You shouldn't have told him. You shouldn't / have said what you said.

ROB: I didn't want to. You know that, right? That I didn't want to? I just.

LUCY: You had to protect Cal.

ROB: Yeah.

LUCY: You used me. (*Beat*) But it's done now, so don't worry about it.

ROB: Lucy.

LUCY: I'll see you on Monday.

(ROB *nods, heads out.*)

DAISY: Hey, don't worry about it, Rob. They'll come around.

ROB: You get home safe, okay, Daisy? It's not safe to walk alone at night. And you've got a long walk home.

(ROB *exits. Beat.* LUCY *looks at the whisky bottle. The lights suddenly go out, and the two are lit only by the ghost light. The place is suddenly awfully dark.*)

DAISY: So, what happened? Did you black out?

LUCY: What do you mean?

DAISY: One minute you're all for releasing it, then. Did you not remember?

LUCY: I remembered.

DAISY: When?

LUCY: At night time, usually. Just before going to bed. It's not like you think, you know? You think it'll be slow and you'll have time to think. You think you'll be brave. It wasn't. I wasn't. I froze.

DAISY: Do you think you could have stopped it?

LUCY: I don't know. But I didn't. (*Beat*) And then when Sarah came in with this tape, I thought, I thought it was like a second chance. A way to make it right. All I'd have to do is keep my mouth shut and raise my hand, you know? I could do the right thing. But then when I saw the way he looked at me. (*Near tears*) Like I was a monster. Like he didn't even know me. He knew me best, he—

DAISY: Yeah, you know what? You should say you blacked out. If anybody asks.

LUCY: Thanks. I should get going. Snow's probably getting pretty bad. *(She goes to exit. Stops)* You know, Daisy, we're not bad people, you know? You know that, right?

*(*DAISY *just looks away.* LUCY *holds the bottle close to her and exits.* APRIL *re-enters and* DAISY *doesn't move.)*

APRIL: Daisy—

DAISY: You know, I'd believe that you'd lie for him. You'd do it for me if I asked you to. I wouldn't even have to ask you. What I don't buy is that you can't even imagine…

APRIL: Daisy.

DAISY: That you don't believe that Cal could have done this. That you'd want to believe? Maybe. And you can lie to them if you want to, you can lie to yourself, even, but don't lie to me.

APRIL: So, what do you want me to say?

DAISY: That you knew what you were doing. That you know what he did.

APRIL: That isn't true.

DAISY: That you knew what happened to her. You just didn't care.

APRIL: That isn't fair, Daisy.

DAISY: Then you cared, just not as much as Liz did about Maggie. Or Malcolm did about Lucy. Or you did about Cal. You threw that girl under the bus. You buried that girl. And I just think you should say it, is all. Just once.

APRIL: Why?

DAISY: Because it's the truth.

APRIL: I mean, why?

DAISY: Because she deserved it. She deserved better.

APRIL: Better than what?

DAISY: Than us. *(Beat)* So, will you say it? Can you say it?

(Beat. APRIL *looks away. Again.* DAISY *starts to get her shit together.)*

DAISY: You know, this? The problem with this, this whole thing? It should have been about her. All of it. But it wasn't. Not for a second. So, I hope it was all worth it, April, I really do.

APRIL: Daisy.

DAISY: What?

*(*APRIL*'s cell phone starts ringing. She looks down at the phone and then back up to her friend. Beat. And once again,* DAISY *realizes* APRIL *isn't going to say anything.)*

DAISY: So, was it worth it?

*(*DAISY *exits. The phone rings and rings until* APRIL *silences it. And now she is alone.)*

*(*APRIL *reaches up and turns off the ghost light.)*

END OF PLAY

CPSIA information can be obtained
at www.ICGtesting.com
Printed in the USA
FFOW01n2150270716
26109FF